MILITARY HISTORY OF THE CHANNEL ISLANDS DURING WORLD WAR II

Table of Contents

Battery Lothringen 1
Granville Raid 3
Hohlgangsanlage 8 4
Hohlgangsanlage tunnels, Jersey 4
Island at War 7
Occupation of the Channel Islands ... 15
Operation Accumulator 21
Operation Ambassador 21
Operation Basalt 23

Preface

Each chapter in this book ends with a URL to a hyperlinked online version. Use the online version to access related pages, websites, footnotes, tables, color photos, updates, or to see the chapter's contributors. Click the edit link to suggest changes. Please type the URL exactly as it appears. If you change the URL's capitalization, for example, it may not work.

Purchase of this book entitles you to a free trial membership in the publisher's book club at www.booksllc.net. (Time limited offer.) Simply enter the barcode number from the back cover onto the membership form on our home page. The book club entitles you to select from millions of books at no additional charge, including a digital copy of this and related books to read on the go. Simply enter the title or subject onto the search form to find them.

If you have any questions, could you please be so kind as to consult our Frequently Asked Questions page at www.booksllc.net/faqs.cfm? You are also welcome to contact us there.

Publisher: Books LLC, Wiki Series, Memphis, TN, USA, 2012.

Battery Lothringen

Battery Lothringen
Part of Atlantic Wall
Noirmont Point, Saint Brélade, Jersey

Battery Lothringen seen from the sea in 2009

Coordinates	
Built	1941
Built by	Organisation Todt
Construction materials	Concrete, steel and timber
In use	1941-45
Current condition	Some structures restored, others ruined
Current owner	People of Jersey
Open to the public	Yes
Garrison	Kriegsmarine
Events	Occupation of the Channel Islands

Kriegsmarine Ensign

Battery Lothringen was a World War II coastal artillery battery in Saint Brélade, Jersey, named after the SMS *Lothringen*, and constructed by Organisation Todt for the Wehrmacht during the Occupation of the Channel Islands. The first installations were completed in 1941, around the same time as the completion of the nearby Battery Moltke, in St. Ouen.

The battery site is located at the end of Noirmont Point, a rock headland which overlooks St. Aubin's Bay, Elizabeth Castle, and the harbours of Saint Helier. It was a part of the Atlantic Wall system of coastal fortifications, and most of the concrete structures remain today.

3rd Battery of Naval Artillery Battalion 604 were stationed here.

Naval guns

In 1941, the main guns in the battery were three 15 cm SK L/45 naval guns, with a fourth 15 cm SK L/45 installed later.

These guns were originally manufactured by Krupp and date from 1917.

The guns were placed on elevated concrete platforms.

Ammunition was stored in nearby bunkers, and was manually transferred from the bunkers, via concrete footpaths, to smaller concrete storage bays at the guns.

After the Liberation of the Channel Islands, the guns were removed by the British Army, and discarded at the foot of the cliffs at Les Landes, in St Ouen.

Gun no. 1

"Gun no. 1" in 2012. The path (right) leads down to Ammunition Bunker VII.

This gun was positioned on top of a walled concrete platform, with one access ramp, and a small room alongside the gun.

Ammunition was stored in Ammunition Bunker VII, and was manually moved from the bunker up to the gun, via a sloping concrete path, to be stowed upright in small bays, just to the rear of the gun.

To the rear of the platform, there was a barrack hut, an administrative building, and a personnel bunker. Only the bunker remains in 2012.

To the east, was a latrine structure.

Electrical and communications services for this gun were linked to the command bunker.

In 1992, the gun no. 1 was recovered and returned Noirmont Point. The recovery work was completed in March 1998, by placing the cannon back on to the gun platform, using a Chinook helicopter.

Gun no. 2

In 1941, this gun was positioned on top of a concrete platform, located to the north east of the command bunker.

Gun no. 3

Gun no. 3 was positioned on top of a concrete platform. The ammunition bunkers are not in close proximity to this platform, so extra storage bays were built below the platform.

In 2012, there is no gun at this position. A section of the platform wall is missing, due to demolition when the gun was removed.

Gun no. 4

Gun no. 4 was positioned on top of a concrete platform.

MP1 tower

MP1 tower with panoramic views.

The Marine Peilstand 1 tower, or MP1 tower, was used to observe targets at

Plaque attached to the tower.

sea. The round tower is around 16 metres (52 ft) tall, and has four observation floors, each with a wide, and short embrasure (for observation purposes only). Each of these floors was assigned to observe for one of the four 15 cm naval guns. The tower has five floors, including a windowless lower floor, plus a further open rooftop floor. Access is gained via a steel door, at the top floor, which is protected by an adjacent embrasure, suitable for small arms.

An Oerlikon 20 mm cannon was placed on the top of the tower for anti-aircraft purposes. In 2012, the gun is no longer present, but its steel support can be seen.

The tower, built between April and October 1943, is located near the top of the steep sloping cliff, and extends no higher than the headland, which means its profile does not protrude in to the sky when seen from afar. The visibility of the tower was reduced further using camouflage.

It is one of three completed direction and range finding towers, of this type, in Jersey. Nine towers were planned, but only towers numbered 1 to 3 were built.

The towers were to be positioned around the entire coast of Jersey, so that any neighboring pair of towers could work together to pin-point a precise location of a target using triangulation. The position of the target would be passed on to the artillery, so that the gun could be rotated, raised or lowered to the correct orientation to fire upon that position.

Westwall type 101v bunker

This personnel bunker is adjacent to the tower. It was sealed and filled in after the Liberation, and was excavated from 2009, by the Channel Islands Occupation Society.

Type M.132 Command bunker

Command bunker at Battery Lothringen. The rangefinder (left), and cupolas (right).

The command bunker is located alongside the MP1 tower. It featured an armored naval rangefinder, and two steel observation cupolas. A periscope was used in conjunction with the rangefinder, to determine the direction of a target.

The bunker was built between March 1943, and May 1944. It has two floors, one entrance, and an escape shaft. It is constructed from reinforced concrete formwork.

The lower-floor serves as a living area, and has 9 chambers, which include quarters for troops, 2 rooms for officers, an administration room, a standyby room, a room for central heating plant, and a coal store. There is an escape shaft, which is accessible from the NCO's room.

The upper-floor includes the operations room, washroom, toilets, first aid room, telephone exchange, and an escape shaft. The main entrance is on this floor, and is defended by two embrasures.

The operations room provides underside access to the cupolas.

In 2012, only the arms of the rangefinder are original, these were recovered from the foot of the cliffs. They were restored and attached to a new turret.

This bunker has been restored, and operates as a museum during the tourist season.

Searchlights

Two searchlights were installed, on concrete platforms, on either side of the headland.

In 2012, only the platforms remain.

Present day

In 2012, the headland site is fully accessible at all times. Some of the installations and interiors are in a restored state, and can be visited at various times - usually on Sundays.

A searchlight platform, at Battery Lothringen, in 2012.

The gun emplacements can be visited at any time, including two partly restored guns, on display, at two of the gun platforms.

There is a public car park at the end of the headland.

Source http://en.wikipedia.org/wiki/Battery_Lothringen

Granville Raid

The **Granville Raid** occurred on the night of 8 March 1945 – 9 March 1945 when a German raiding force from the Channel Islands landed in Allied-occupied France and brought back supplies to their base.

History

During the Second World War, Granville, Manche, France was the site of a prisoner of war camp. In December 1944 four German paratroopers and a Naval cadet escaped from the camp, eventually stole an American LCVP landing craft, and made their way to the German occupied Channel Islands. They were greeted as heroes and reported that several ships were in the harbour at Granville discharging coal, which was in short supply in the beleaguered Islands. They also reported the disposition of American troops in the area. The former prisoners had been shot down by a night fighter when returning to Germany in early 1945.

The new garrison commander of the Channel Islands, Admiral Friedrich Hüffmeier, a former captain of the German battleship Scharnhorst, used the intelligence to plan a raid against the Allies to restore morale to his garrison and obtain needed supplies. An early raid on the night of 6 February 1945 – 7 February 1945 was called off by a combination of bad weather and when an escorting *Schnellboot* was detected by US Navy submarine chaser PC-552.

The successful raid, led by *Kapitänleutnant* Carl-Friedrich Mohr, occurred on the night of 8 March 1945 – 9 March 1945. Hüffmeier's raiding force comprised four large M class minesweepers (*M-412*, *M-432*, *M-442*, *M-459*), three armed barges (artillery lighters) carrying 88mm cannons, three fast motor launches, two small R type minesweepers, and a seagoing tug. Though the raid was successful in its execution, Allied resistance delayed the time table so only one collier, the *Eskwood* containing 112 tonnes of coal, could be taken back to the Channel Islands due to the low tide. A German minesweeper, the M-412 *De Schelde*, ran aground, being eventually blown up by the Germans.

While on patrol outside the harbor, an American submarine chaser, PC 564, faced with a jammed 3 inch gun and overwhelmed by the large German flotilla, was seriously damaged, with the pilot house blown off and many crew killed or injured. The order was given to abandon ship and several crew did so, later being taken POWs. The captain, Lt. Percy Sandel, then intentionally grounded the vessel while evading the Germans. After sending a crew member ashore to find help, captain and remaining crew aboard were later picked up by allied forces and PC 564 was salvaged, remaining in the US Naval registry until 1963.

The Germans mined and badly damaged the British freighters *Kyle Castle*, *Nephrite*, *Parkwood* and the Norwegian merchantman *Heien* but they remained aground at low tide. The Captain of the *Kyle Castle* refused to cooperate and was killed - Richard Reed took over as Captain, hid with another until the Germans retired, and managed to repair the hull damage at its shallow location some way out of harbour. With engines unusable, he floated the ship out on the ebb tide south of the Channel Isles and with the aid of hatch covers as sails, managed to make the Channel and was towed into Plymouth. German forces also damaged the locks and harbour and started fires. Several American prisoners were taken (some sources claim 30 allied servicemen were taken, Including 15 of the crew of PC 564) and 55 German POWs were liberated (some sources claim 67). Two US marines were killed at the hotel, and with the help of the hotel staff the Germans rounded up the nine most senior US personnel in the town. About 14 US seamen from the submarine chaser were killed in action. One RN officer and five of his men also died during this attack.

Mohr was awarded the Knight's Cross on 13 March 1945 with *Oberleutnant zur See* Otto Karl in command of Artillery Lighter AF 65 was awarded the Knights Cross on 21 March 1945.

Later raids

In a later operation, an 18-man German sabotage raid from Jersey landing from rubber boats on Cape de la Hague on 5 April 1945 with a mission to destroy installations failed. They were captured.

A further raid was planned for 7 May 1945, but Admiral Karl Dönitz ordered Hüffmeier not to carry out any more offensive operations so close to the end of the war.

Source http://en.wikipedia.org/wiki/Granville_Raid

Hohlgangsanlage 8

Hohlangsanlage 8
German Underground Hospital
Part of Atlantic Wall
Jersey

Entrance to Ho8

Built	1941 - 1945
Built by	Organisation Todt
Construction materials	Concrete, steel, and tim
In use	1941-45
Current condition	Restored, museum & m ial to slave labourers
Open to the public	Yes
Events	Occupation of the Chan Islands

Flag of Germany 1933-45

Hohlgangsanlage 8 (often abbreviated to **Ho8**, also known as the **German Underground Hospital** or the **Jersey War Tunnels**) was a partially completed underground hospital complex in St. Lawrence, Jersey, built by German occupying forces during the occupation of Jersey during World War II. Over 1 km (1,100 yd) of tunnels were completed. After the liberation of the Channel Islands, the complex was converted into a museum detailing the occupation and remains a visitor attraction.

History

After Hitler's October 1941 order to fortify the Channel Islands (as part of the Atlantic Wall), work began on a string of fortifications all around Jersey. Ho8 was intended to be a vast network of underground tunnels that would allow the German occupying infantry to withstand Allied air raids and bombardment (in preparation for an invasion). Forced labourers from the Organisation Todt (as well as paid labourers and skilled workers) were shipped in to Jersey and put to work building the complex. Many of the workers were Polish, French, Russian or Republican Spaniards. Conditions were terrible, although Russian and Ukrainian POWs were treated the worst, with cases of malnutrition, death by exhaustion and disease among them becoming common. On the other hand, the voluntary workers often had much better conditions, being offered over four times the wages that they would have earned working in similar jobs for the States of Jersey, and often receiving extra food rations.

In late 1943, with the threat of an Allied invasion of Europe (Operation Overlord) becoming clear, Ho8 was to be converted into a casualty clearing station and emergency hospital. The hospital had 500 beds for patients, with a full heating and air conditioning system (although the rest of tunnel complex usually maintained a constant temperature of about 17 °C (63 °F), due to its being built deep into the hillside). A system of gas-proof doors was installed to maintain a clean airflow in the tunnels, and a fully equipped operating theatre was installed. The hospital was intended only for German military casualties in an invasion — no civilian casualties would have been treated. Unfinished tunnels were sealed off.

Despite the huge preparations and fortifications made to the Channel Islands, none were ever put into practice. The occupying forces in the Channel Islands surrendered on 9 May 1945 (one day after the rest of the German forces surrendered). Ho8 fell into disuse, with British soldiers and souvenir hunters stripping the tunnels of equipment.

Post-liberation & Present Day

In July 1946, the States of Jersey opened the tunnels to the public. In 1961, the Royal Court ruled that the subterranean complex belonged to the private owners of the land above it, and Ho8 fell under private ownership. The complex was restored, with a collection of Occupation memorabilia and a museum and memorial to the occupation being set up. In 2001, a permanent exhibit called "Captive Island" was unveiled in the tunnel complex, detailing everyday life for civilians in Jersey before, during and after the occupation of Jersey. Today, Ho8 is generally referred to as the "Jersey War Tunnels". The Jersey War Tunnels has also housed military vehicles such as a Char B1 bis tank, which served in Jersey with the Panzer-Abteilung 213 during the occupation which was on loan from the Bovington Tank Museum. As of March 2012 there is also a replica Stug III tank destroyer owned by the war tunnels.

Source http://en.wikipedia.org/wiki/Hohlgangsanlage_8

Hohlgangsanlage tunnels, Jersey

Hohlgangsanlagen   *German Tunnels*   Part of Atlantic Wall

Jersey

The northern-most entrance to Ho2 in S

Built	1941-1945
Built by	Festungsbaubattalione, /Gesteinsbar Btl. 77, R beitsdienst, Organisatic various contractors Gei local
Construction materials	Concrete, steel, and tin
Demolished	Some (by both Germar British
Current condition	One fully restored, othe tained, most abandonec
Current owner	Owner of land above tu
Open to the public	One open to the public be visited with land ow mission.
Controlled by	States & private owner
Events	Occupation of the Char

Flag of the German occupying forces

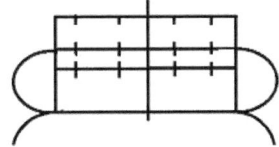

Plan of Ho2 a ration store, tunnels were built to similar designs depending on their intended use

Hohlgangsanlage are a number of tunnels constructed in Jersey by occupying German forces during the Occupation of Jersey. The Germans intended these

This rail tunnel formed the entrance to Ho5

The main entrance of Ho8

bunkers to protect troops and equipment from aerial bombing and to act as fortifications in their own right.

The word *Hohlgangsanlage* can be translated as "cave passage installations". The Channel Island tunnels are the only ones on the Atlantic wall to be referred to as *Hohlganganlagen*.

All the tunnels except for Ho5 are incomplete, and some never progressed beyond planning. The partly complete tunnels are, nonetheless, substantial in

Central section of Ho2

A tunnel in Ho8

size. Completed sections were used for various purposes such as storage.

In 1944, when construction stopped, 244,000 m of rock had been extracted collectively from Guernsey, Jersey and Alderney (the majority from Jersey). At the same point in 1944 the entire Atlantic Wall from Norway to the Franco-Spanish border, excluding the Channel Islands, had extracted some 225,000 m.

History 1941-present day

Tunnel construction began in 1941, shortly before Hitler's October 1941 decree that the islands be defended. The tunnels were constructed at strategic points around the island. Most of the tunnels were for shelter or storage, but some were used as part of and to link fortifications in strong points (such as at

Corbière) and were part of casemates. The tunnels were constructed by the *Festungsbaubattalione* (fortress construction battalions), *4/Gesteinbohr Btl. 77* (specialist mining battalions), the RAD (state labour for 17-18 year olds) and the Organisation Todt. In 1941 Fritz Todt came to inspect the progress of the fortifications. The Germans used a variety of labour sources, most being forced. After Todt's death Albert Speer drastically reduced the resources available for the construction of tunnels on the island. During 1944 there was a shortage of raw materials, so effort was diverted to finish only the most complete tunnels. On May 9, 1945, construction stopped with the liberation of Jersey.

Immediately after the war, the British used the tunnels: soon after the Liberation of the Channel Islands, some military equipment was moved and stored in the tunnels. For example, Ho1 stored anti aircraft guns, Ho2 stored small equipment such as helmets, fuel, and oxyacetylene. Ho13 stored Panzer Abteilung 213's Char B1 bis tanks.

During the 1950s scrap metal drive they were mostly cleared and sealed. Under Jersey law, a landowner owns everything beneath his land, down to the centre of the earth; so all the tunnels are privately owned. *Hohlgangsanlage 8* is the only tunnel open to the public without special permission from the land owner; it was opened to the public in 1946 by the British army, then gifted to the States of Jersey by the War Department. After a lawsuit by the owners of the land above, it became privately owned but still operates as a museum today.

Post 1962 all the tunnels were thoroughly cleared of German equipment (apart from the museum, Ho1 due to roof collapse and Ho4 due to masses of barbed wire, roof collapses and unexploded ordnance) after a tragedy in which two souvenir hunters died of carbon monoxide poisoning in Ho2.

The tunnels are very unstable as, contrary to popular belief, most were bored not into solid granite, but loose shale. This is evident from the large number of roof collapses in the incomplete unlined tunnels. Most of the tunnels still survive today and are infrequently visited by organised parties (with permission).

There were plans to use some of the tunnels during the Swine flu pandemic; fortunately the pandemic never materialised.

Construction and design

The tunnels were dug into the sides of hills, into rock. This means that incomplete tunnels remain mostly intact, due to the strength of the unsupported rock. Completed sections are lined with concrete floors, walls, and ceilings.

There was a basic design of storage and personnel tunnel. Storage tunnels incorporated a 60 cm gauge railway in a loop running around the whole complex and a small platform for loading supplies; they usually had two entrances so that vehicles could continuously enter and exit the complex. Personnel tunnels were built like a grid; the railway was often removed after construction was complete. Completed tunnels would have been lined in concrete, and have drainage, lighting and air conditioning systems.

In all, 19-25 storage tunnels were planned, but due to the almost wholesale destruction of primary source material before the surrender the exact number is unknown (although the number where work began is known).

Where possible, the tunnel routes avoided granite and instead they were routed through looser shale rock formations. The tunnels were dug by the traditional method of drilling and blasting. When the tunnels were bored out they were lined with concrete. First the floor was lined, followed by the walls and finally the roof. The walls were concreted using wooden shuttering, the space between the shuttering and the rock face was filled with concrete, and the shuttering subsequntly removed. The roof was made in the same way, but using curved shuttering balancing on the concrete walls. Concrete was poured down the escape shafts rather than through the tunnel entrances to avoid contamination with the rock leaving the tunnel; these shoots can still be seen in many of the tunnels. Contrary to popular belief there were relatively few accidents and deaths in the building programme itself, but many slave labourers died of starvation.

The tunnels

Storage Tunnels *Tunnels used only for storage*

Ho1 - Munitions store - West side of La Route d'Aleval - Incomplete but used, recently used as a mushroom farm

Ho2 – Ration store – East side of La Route d'Aleval - Incomplete

Ho3 – Munitions store - Planning stage only.

Ho4 - Munitions store - West side of Grand Vaux Valley - Incomplete but used (now used by Jersey Water for storage).

Ho5 – Fuel store - St. Aubin, Railway Walk - Complete, but used for munitions, now in use by the states.

Ho6 - Personnel shelter – L'Aleval, exact location unknown - Unknown if ever got past exploratory stage

Ho7 – Artillery reserves – Cap Verd - Exploratory work only (rear entrance to Ho8 is also here)

Ho8 - Artillery quarters - St Peter's Valley & Cap Verd - Incomplete but converted to hospital, and now a visitor attraction

Ho9 - Electricity works – Bellozanne Valley - Planning stage only

Ho10 - Ration store – Grands Vaux, between Mont Neron and Ruisseaux - Incomplete

Ho11 - Personnel shelter - Planning stage only

Ho12 - Fuel store – La Commune - Exploratory work only.

Ho13 - Munition store - East side Beaumont Valley – Incomplete.

Ho14 - Fuel store – Planning stage only.

Ho15 - Store - West side of Beaumont Valley - Incomplete

Ho16 – Personnel Shelter - West side of Beaumont Valley at road level – Incomplete, abandoned (not known if still in existence).

Ho17 - Unknown - Unknown.

Ho18 - Hospital - Westmout, disued mine/civilian air raid shelter - Planning

Stage Only.

Ho19 - Electricity works – first entrance from town La Folie, St Helier - Incomplete, used by States.

Ho20 - Tunnel- Mount Bingham - Incomplete

Ho21 - Stores - Jubilee Hill - Planning Stage

Ho22 - Stores - Rozel Valley - Planning Stage

Ho23 - Personnel Shelter - Grouville Marsh - Planning Stage

Ho24/25 - Greve de Lecq Valley/St. Ouen - Planning Stage

Railway Tunnels *Tunnels designed only for use as railway tunnels*

Eastern Railway Connecting tunnel - 2nd entrance at La Folie under Mt. Bingham - Incomplete, in use by JEC

Fortified Tunnels Either stand alone or as part of emplacements

Ho Etaquerel - Casemate complex - L'Etacq, St. Ouen - Completed

Ho Mole Verclut - Casemate complex - Verclut Point (Gibraltar Rock) - Completed now in use by Jersey Turbot

Stützpunkt Doktorhaus - Personnel Bunker with Machine Gun post - Mont Matthieu St. Ouen - Completed

Stützpunkt Corbiere - Communications tunnel between bunkers - La Corbiere - Completed, bunkers open to the public by CIOS

Batterie Derfflinger - Gun battery with accomadtion - Le Mont de la Rocque, St. Brelade - completed

Batterie Seydlitz - Gun battery with accomadtion - Le Mont du Coin, St Brelade

Batterie Moltke - Gun battery with tunnel system - Les Landes Common, St Ouen - completed, open to public by CIOS

Batterie Schliefen - Small wood lined tunnel - Verclut, Grouville - lost

Associated with tunnels *Infrastructure used to support tunnels*

Stream Culvert *(not a V1 launch ramp!)*- Beaumont Valley (used to protect stream from planned dumping of rubble)- intact visible from road

Stone Crusher - L'Aleval, between Ho2 entrances - ruins

Power Station - St Peter's Valley, Tesson Mill area - Main building and reservoir can be seen from road

Queens Road Power Station - Queens Road - Used to supply electricity to the whole Island including tunnels (tunnels would also have backup generators)

Source http://en.wikipedia.org/wiki/Hohlgangsanlage_tunnels,_Jersey

Island at War

Island at War

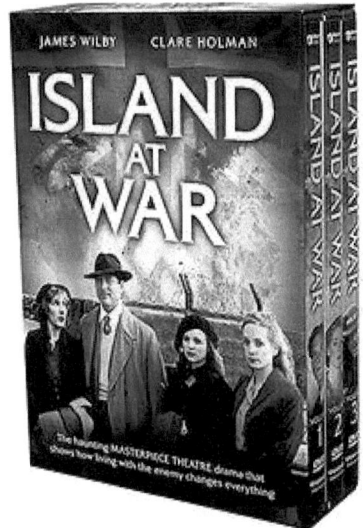

Format	Drama
Written by	Stephen Mallatratt
Starring	James Wilby
	Clare Holman
	Owen Teale
	Julia Ford
	Philip Glenister
	Saskia Reeves
Country of origin	🇬🇧 United Kingdom
No. of episodes	6 (UK) (List of episodes)
Production	
Executive producer(s)	Sita Williams
	Andy Harries
Running time	approx. 398 min
Broadcast	
Original channel	ITV (ITV1/STV/UTV)
Original airing	11 July 2004
External links	
(US) Website	

Island at War is a British television series that tells the story of the German Occupation of the Channel Islands. It primarily focuses on three local families: the upper class Dorrs, the middle class Mahys and the working class Jonases, and four German officers. The fictional island of St. Gregory serves as a stand-in for the real-life islands Jersey and Guernsey, and the story is compiled from the events on both islands.

Produced by Granada Television in Manchester, *Island at War* had an estimated budget of £9,000,000 and was filmed on location in the Isle of Man from August 2003 to October 2003.

When the series was shown in the UK, it appeared in six 70-minute episodes.

Cast of characters

The islanders

James Dorr

James Dorr is a member of the St. Gregory Senate, and is deputy bailiff of the island's government. His family is well-known and respected; both his father and grandfather have served as Bailiff. He loves his wife Felicity, but cannot be sure she loves him and often finds that she gets in his way. He sent his son Phillip to England to go to boarding school, something that Felicity never quite forgave him for.

James takes his job in the Senate very seriously, and works hard to ensure that the transition into occupation is as painless as possible for his fellow islanders. He knows full well that the Germans are capable of killing every person on St. Gregory, and encourages his friends and family to avoid stirring up the waters for fear of German retaliation. He is suspicious of his wife's relationship with Baron Von Rheingarten, and doesn't trust either of them completely. When Phillip and La Salle arrive on St. Gregory to gather information, James worries that their presence may invite resistance; his sense of duty to St. Gregory tends to cloud his judgment.

James Dorr was played by James Wilby.

Felicity Dorr

Felicity is James Dorr's wife. Not a native of St. Gregory, she was born and educated in England, where she met James. She and James conceived a child the night they met, and were married very quickly afterward. Felicity does not terribly enjoy living on St. Gregory, finding island life boring and stuffy. She is, however, very devoted to her husband James, especially after the occupation begins. Felicity does not quite share her husband's loyalty to St. Gregory itself, but rather to her friends and family on the island.

Felicity is good friends with Urban Mahy; the two perform in a theatre troupe on St. Gregory (known as Am-Drams, a commonly used *portmanteau* of amateur dramatics).

Felicity misses her son Phillip terribly, and is delighted when he returns to St. Gregory to gather information for the war effort. She forms a rather uneasy friendship with Baron Von Rheingarten, and the two often sit outside at night and talk. This makes James suspicious of both of them, despite Felicity's refusal of the Baron's advances. When the Baron discovers that 'Mr Brotherson' is in fact Felicity's son, she offers herself to him in return for him sparing her son's life. The Baron rejects her 'proposal' but does see to it that Philip is not killed.

Felicity Dorr was played by Clare Holman.

Phillip Dorr (aka Mr. Brotherson)

Philip Dorr is the only son of James and Felicity. He was educated, like his father before him, at Stowe. He went directly into the army, where he's in training at Sandhurst. Philip loves his parents but sometimes finds himself caught between them.

When Philip is sent back to the island as a spy on a reconnaissance mission, he adopts the persona of "Mr. Brotherson" and becomes an odd-job man at his parents' house, 'Sous Les Chenes.' His belief in the power of the Allies comes into conflict with James' determination to protect the people of St. Gregory.

In the final episode he is caught trying to escape back to Britain with information and photos of the German military installations on the island. His life is spared by the Baron but he is sent to France as a prisoner of war.

Phillip Dorr was played by Sam Heughan.

Wilf Jonas

Wilf is the local policeman who feels a genuine sense of duty, bringing him into conflict with some of his colleagues. He's a bit of a gambler and risk taker, and enjoys the adventure and uncertainty of his job. He loathes paperwork, loves his wife and despises his brother-in-law. Wilf also likes to fish the local waters around the island of St. Gregory.

He is eventually forced to be driver for Oberst Heinrich Baron Von Rheingarten; something which he detests even more than the paperwork associated with being a policeman.

He assists the escape attempt of Philip Dorr and Zelda Kay, but is caught and sent to prison in France for 6–9 months.

Wilf Jonas was played by Owen Teale.

Kathleen Jonas

Wilf's wife is high energy. She loves to run the farm, and to clean and cook for her family. She shares Wilf's sense of what's right and wrong up to a point, but is more willing to bend the rules, especially when her brother, Sheldon Leveque is involved. She's adventurous and always ready for fun. She puts her husband and two children before herself and will keep secrets from Wilf if she feels it necessary.

When the island authorities recommend evacuating children from the island, Kathleen make the heart-wrenching decision to send her 2 children, Colin and Mary, to England to be safe.

Kathleen assists Philip Dorr and Eugene La Salle when they return to the island as spies, despite the danger it puts herself and her family in.

Kathleen was born on 22 January 1904 and used to be a Sunday School Teacher.

Kathleen Jonas was played by Julia Ford.

Sheldon Leveque

Sheldon is Kathleen's brother and a handsome charmer who can talk himself out of any situation. It's never quite clear how he makes his living. He appears to be a crafty wheeler-dealer who manages to work both for and against the Germans. He's also one of the few islanders allowed to keep a vehicle, although no one is quite sure why.

He spends a lot of time in the Jonas household and is genuinely fond of his sister, but less so of Wilf. In fact, as soon as Wilf arrives home, Sheldon finds an excuse to leave. He makes it his business to know everyone, believing they may be useful to him one day.

Sheldon Leveque was played by Sean Gallagher.

Cassie Mahy

Cassie runs a successful grocery store which she inherited from her parents. This makes her the main breadwinner in the family. She adores her husband Urban who acknowledges that she has the business brain of the partnership. She's a bit older than he is but she'll defer to him in matters of their children's upbringing.

After her husband was killed during the German invasion, she detests the Germans and everything they stand for, but that doesn't stop her working with them when it suits her. She begins a business partnership (and later a sexual relationship) with German Oberwachtmeister Wimmel.

Cassie Mahy was played by Saskia Reeves.

Urban Mahy

Urban Mahy is the near-polar opposite of his wife Cassie. Urban is a genial chap with an easy-going attitude who's content to go along with whatever comes his way. He feels lucky to have his wife Cassie, and is delighted by his children. His wife inherited the grocery store from her parents and Every so often he has a twinge of conscience because Cassie is the family breadwinner. This leads him to a crisis of conscience. He is delighted, therefore, when Mr. Isaaks offers to give his camera shop to Urban when the former evacuates St. Gregory. He is several years younger than Cassie, but she acknowledges him as the head of the household. Urban loves Cassie deeply, but they often disagree on issues such as business and child-rearing.

He is good friends with Felicity Dorr, and the two are members of the local thespian club, *"AmDrams"*.

Urban was killed when the Germans bombed the harbour during their invasion, and was buried in an unmarked grave.

Urban Mahy was played by Julian Wadham.

Angelique Mahy

Angelique is the elder of Urban and Cassie Mahy's two daughters. She works at the Government house as an assistant to James Dorr and the Bailiff La Palotte. Compared to her sister June, Angelique is much more aggressive toward the Germans. She is absolutely against their presence on St. Gregory, and refuses to cooperate with them when she can. When she and June take over Mr. Isaaks' camera shop, Angelique is against removing the former owner's name from the store window, as it would mean having to cater to the German soldiers.

She has a strong sense of morality and will be the first to challenge her sister or mother if she thinks they are out of line. This makes life very complicated for her when she finds herself in a dubious moral situation: she falls for German airman Bernhardt Tellemann. Because Angelique cares so much about what others - especially her mother and sister - think of her, she initially refuses to admit her feelings to herself, but eventually gives into them and embarks on a relationship with him.

Angelique Mahy was played by Joanne Froggatt.

June Mahy

June, the younger of Urban and Cassie Mahy's two daughters, is seventeen. She is impressionable, a bit of a daddy's girl, and younger than her years. She's in the amateur dramatic society, and sings at the 50/50 Club, which is taken over by Germans. When the Germans arrive, June truly does not know how to act. Her mother and sister believe that the Germans are evil and to be avoided, June cannot help but treat them like ordinary people. Being friendly with the Germans eventually gets June into trouble, and she becomes branded a "Jerrybag" by some of her fellow islanders.

June Mahy was played by Samantha Robinson.

Zelda Kay

Zelda Kay (real name: "Hannah Kosminski") is a German Jew who escaped the country with her mother in 1933. They settled in England, where Zelda found work as a nanny. The family she worked for often spent their summers in St. Gregory, and that's where Zelda found herself when war broke out in September 1939. Since she was a German national, she was not allowed back into Britain. Stranded on St. Gregory, Mr. Isaaks befriended her, gave her a job in his shop and found a flat for her to rent.

As a German invasion becomes more of a certainty, Zelda makes arrangements to evacuate St. Gregory, but ultimately misses the last boat. Stranded again, she continues to work in the camera shop, though now for Angelique and June Mahy. As a Jewish woman living among Nazi soldiers, Zelda tries very hard to keep her secret. Unfortunately, she catches the eye of Oberleutnant Walker, and must continually reject his advances. As the occupation continues, Zelda must go into hiding to avoid her secret being made known.

Once her identity is discovered by Walker, he forces her into a sexual relationship in exchange for keeping her secret. She decides she must escape the island and tries to do so by boat, alongside Philip Dorr. Their boat is discovered by the Germans, but Zelda jumps overboard, returns to the island and goes back into hiding.

Zelda Kay was played by Louisa Clein.

The Germans

Baron Heinrich Von Rheingarten

Oberst (Colonel) Baron Heinrich Von Rheingharten is a married man with two sons in the Luftwaffe. He first appears in the last scenes of the first episode, and quickly establishes that he is a man of aristocracy. He is the commandant of the island of St. Gregory, in charge of everything that happens there, along with Captain Muller and Leutnant Walker.

Von Rheingarten is not a Nazi in the true sense of the word; he is just loyal to his army and his country. He's also no pushover. He will not be made to look a fool and isn't afraid of making tough decisions, but he understands the frailties of human nature.

He takes an interest in Mrs. Dorr, making conversation with her a few times, after shunning the attempts of her husband, and also shows almost paternal affections for Mr. Brotherson (Phillip Dorr) and spends a bit of episode 2 walling with him. When Eugene La Salle is found to be a spy, he is the one to order his execution, as retaliation for the killing of one of his soldiers. He also claims that the island needs a death to remind them who is in charge, and that it will prevent further spying.

In the final episode he finds that his youngest son, Manfred, was shot down over the Channel, and says to Mrs. Dorr "Maybe she (his wife) does not know and is picking out a star for him now." When she brings up La Salle's mother, he remarks, "One only does what one thinks is right," and that whoever shot down his son was right and would be congratulated.

When Phillip Dorr (a.k.a. Mr. Brotherson) is caught with photos of the German facilities, Mrs. Dorr reveals to him that Mr. Brotherson is actually her son, Phillip, and offers herself to him in order to save her son. He spares her son from execution, instead sending him to France as a prisoner of war, along with his driver Wilf Jonas and James Dorr, who will attend a prison for at least 9 months for assisting him. When Mrs. Dorr thanks him he replies, "I have grown sickened by young men dying".

Baron Von Rheingarten was played by Philip Glenister.

Captain Muller
Captain Muller was played by Daniel Flynn (actor).

Oberleutnant Walker
Lieutenant Walker is a complex character. His politics are much further left (socialist/statist) than Von Rheingarten's; he agrees with Hitler's most extreme views. He detests the Jews and enjoys the power he has as a superior officer in an occupying army. However, he is also terribly lonely and desperate to find friendship and love.

He takes a liking to Zelda Kay, not realising she is in fact a German Jew. When he discovers her true identity he tells her he will keep her secret and coerces her into sleeping with him as a thank you.

Oberleutnant Walker was played by Conor Mullen.

Oberleutnant Flach
Oberleutnant Flach was played by Andrew Havill.

Airman Bernhardt Tellemann
Bernhardt was studying for a law degree when war broke out and he was called into the army. He is a navigator in the Luftwaffe; he is responsible for pressing the button that drops the bombs. He is on the deadly harbor raid that announces the Germans' arrival. Despite his youth, Bernhardt has a clear understanding of the horrific situation. He despises Hitler's views, but he is trapped in his army.

He is immediately attracted to Angelique Mahy and the two of them begin a relationship.

Bernhardt Tellemann was played by Laurence Fox.

Minor characters

Eugene La Salle
Eugene La Salle was played by Richard Dempsey.

Ada Jonas
Ada Jonas was played by Ann Rye.

Colin Jonas
Colin Jonas was played by Sean Ward.

Episode synopses

Episode One: Eve of the War
In the opening scene a St. Gregory fisherman (later revealed to be PC Wilf Jonas) is lobstering off the coast of Normandy in his fishing boat called 'Little Mary' when he encounters a British patrol fleeing the Battle of Dunkirk. He agrees to rescue them but as the soldiers swim to his boat they are cut down by German machine-gun fire.

Back at the St. Gregory Parliament, the Bailiff is reassuring the senate that France's surrender to Nazi Germany (June 18, 1940) and the occupation of the Cotentin Peninsula, just 8 miles across the channel, will not affect life on agrarian St. Gregory when it is announced that the British, rather than reinforcing their garrison, are withdrawing completely to leave the island defenceless. The showing of the newsreel of the Wehrmacht marching beneath the Arc de Triomphe, sparks public and private debate whether to remain as patriots ("fleeing would be treachery") or evacuate by boat to safety in England.

As the German invasion looms the aging Bailiff and Senator Dorr speak from the balcony of Parliament, urging calm but neither endorsing nor discouraging an official evacuation. The news strains (or breaks) family relations among the Dorrs, Mahys and Jonases, and erodes social order; looting and profiteering take hold and there is a run on the bank.

Tragedy strikes when the Luftwaffe, having mistaken the tomato lorries parked by the pier for troop carriers, strafes and bombs the port, killing several dozen, including Urban Mahy. A German reconnaissance plane then drops leaflets announcing the protocol for the island's surrender: white flags hung from every structure.

The Dorrs, now reconciled, the Mahys, led by the widow Cassie, and the Jonases, having discovered that their son still on the island (only the daughter evacuated), await the German occupation with the resolve to carry on.

In the final sequence we meet Baron Heinrich Von Rheingarten, the German Commandant who arrives with a battalion of landsers to take possession of St. Gregory "in the name of the Chancellor of the Third Reich". He quickly establishes his credentials as a cultured member of the old Prussian aristocracy, through his courteous treatment of his presumptive peers, the Dorrs, and an appreciation for the local architecture. An efficient officer, he wastes no time in requisitioning the Bailiff's car and "finest hotel on the island" (the St. George) for his staff.

In the final scene he addresses the assembled German troops from the balcony of the Parliament building, now draped in swastikas. His Nazi salute and accompanying "Heil Hitler" strike an ominous note and close the episode.

Episode Two: Living with the Enemy
In general, the episode introduces the German-islander interpersonal relationships to be developed. The opening shots comprise a montage of island life under occupation: Urban Mahy's funeral procession behind a handcart, the Dorrs getting around on bicycles, soldiers smoking in the main square. In a scene reminiscent of Hal Ashby's "Harold and Maude", a marching band, playing Jaromir Vejvoda's "Beer Barrel Polka", passes below the church just as Urban Mahy is being interred. As the music cannot be ignored, June Mahy, his daughter, begins to sing along hesitantly, then with growing conviction as first her mother, followed by the other mourners, join in. The moment is transformed from maudlin to poignant.

The first meeting of Baron Heinrich Von Rheingarten and Senator James Dorr follows, setting up their ideological and personal conflict as one of the series' major themes. Their respective agenda: redressing grievances (Dorr) and acknowledgment of Germans' humanity/superiority (Von Rheingarten), while not mutually exclusive, find them initially talking at cross-purposes.

Urban Mahy's wake provides the opportunity for dialogue framing secondary plot-lines: Sheldon Leveque attempts to ingratiate himself with Cassie Mahy, whose cooperation will abet his war profiteering. Cassie in turn accuses Felicity Dorr of pursuing an affair with her late husband; the handsome Captain Muller arrives with two landsers and impresses June Mahy by having them apologise to the family for accosting them in the street. Meanwhile on the cliff overlooking a secluded beach, Baron Von Rheingarten impresses upon Senator Dorr the rigour of German military discipline: "My men whom you see now frolicking below would slaughter each other in a minute if I so ordered it". They return to the Dorr residence where Felicity Dorr snubs the Baron's social advances. He retaliates by requisitioning the unused wing of their home for himself and senior staff. This begins the Baron Von Rheingarten/James Dorr rivalry for Felicity's attentions, fueled in part by James' confronting her privately with his own false suspicions about an affair with Urban Mahy.

The clandestine arrival of the Dorr son, Phillip, and compatriot Eugene La Salle, now both recruited as British reconnaissance agents, brings the war home to the island. Masquerading as "Mr. Brotherson", a day-labourer on his parents' estate, Phillip quickly finds himself repairing a garden wall alongside the Baron who displays an almost paternal affection for the young man.

After Cassie Mahy refuses to sell groceries to German soldiers, she must face Leutnant Walker who purports to teach her a lesson in the economics of occupation. Intimating that food is scarce throughout Europe, he challenges her on moral grounds. He is also responsible for promulgating Nazi anti-semitic agenda on the island. Not all the Germans are evil, however, and we soon meet Airman Bernhardt Telleman, who urges the Mahy daughters, now running a camera shop they inherited when its Jewish owner evacuated, to serve German soldiers because "we are people too". After convincing the girls to accept his business, he is visibly pleased to formally introduce himself merely as "Bernhardt" and crosses the street with a bounce in his step.

The Baron and Felicity share a frank, almost intimate, moment in the Dorr garden. With faces bathed in moon and lamplight, he offers her chocolates but warns her that his soldiers are "an invading army - men without women" who will sooner or later become "ravenous wolves".

The episode closes on a note of violence: Eugene and Phillip, having completed their reconnaissance mission, are awaiting extraction by submarine on the beach, when they encounter, and kill, a landser on patrol. The machine-gun fire raises the alarm and the pair must conceal the body and evade capture in a house-to-house search mounted by the Germans. Phillip guides Eugene, suffering from hypothermia, to refuge in the Jonas' barn. Again the Baron has the last word to the Dorrs, "I cannot tell you how serious this is - I should hope this doesn't mean .. resistance".

Episode Three: To Catch a Spy

With most of the garrison mobilised to find the missing landser, Wilf Jonas takes the body out on his fishing boat the 'Little Mary' dumping it in deep water. Upon his return to port we meet *Oberleutnant Flach*, the presumptive political officer whose suspicions are aroused by such a long voyage, ostensibly to set lobster pots. Phillip and the now-feverish Eugene remain in hiding in the Jonas barn; a perilous situation, Wilf explains to Felicity, "it is only a matter of time" before they are found, consigning the family to death for harbouring an enemy agent.

Invited to a special session of the Senate, the Baron snubs the Bailiff's attempt to appease him and forestall a reprisal, "ten islanders killed for every German life", and promises to "shoot on sight anyone found on the beaches (at night)". Back at the Dorr residence, now serving as his HQ, he cautions them privately, "We (are not) playing at war".

After stealing German uniforms from the beach, young Colin Jonas runs into an alley where his uncle Sheldon is attempting to sell a car of dubious provenance to *Oberwachtmeister Wimmel*, the German quartermaster sergeant. Back at the camera shop, Lieutenant Walker meets, and is instantly enamoured with, Zelda Kay. Unaware of her Jewish heritage he insists that she accompany him to the officers' party at the 50/50 Club. Under the guise of patronising the camera shop Bernhardt pursues a courtship with Angelique.

When Felicity Dorr visits her son Phillip and Eugene La Salle at the Jonas' barn, it affords an opportunity to share a moment of maternal sympathy with Kathleen, Wilf's wife. Bernhardt Telleman again visits the camera shop but Zelda is there instead and tells him that the German air-raid on the port killed Angelique's father. He buys flowers to lay at the grave and, as luck would have it, finds her also at the cemetery. When she ignores him he chastises her: "...you won't see past the uniform..I studied law, I am not a... fighting man..do you think I want to kill your people?"

That evening at the 50/50 Club, Lieutenant Walker, having forced Zelda to accompany him, tries in vain to create the mood of a double date when he is joined by Captain Dieter Muller and June, who sings regularly at the club. Meanwhile James and Felicity Dorr try to persuade Eugene La Salle to "hand himself in to the German military" as prisoner of war having escaped from occupied France.

The next morning Wilf is conscripted to serve as the Baron's chauffeur while Sheldon traffics in black market produce. Oberwachtmeister Wimmel wants in on the profits and blackmails Cassie into a partnership.

That afternoon Felicity finds the Baron in her garden, when she accuses him of having "no respect for our privacy". "There's a corner of my vineyard," he replies, "which has a wall that was once part of an abbey. I sit there late at night, always alone." The arrival of Senator Dorr breaks the mood and the Baron confronts him with his suspicions about Eugene La Salle's true identity, obtained by Captain Muller from Ada,

Wilf Jonas' mother. Again the Baron has the last word, indirectly implicating Phillip in an espionage plot.

Episode Four: Strange Mercies
At the barracks prison Oberleutnant Flach interrogates and tortures Eugene La Salle, based on an inadvertent tip from Wilf Jonas' mother who saw the "spitting image of Eugene and another boy" in her tomato fields. Eugene doesn't break and the Baron will not let Flach use force on Senator Dorr, Kathleen Jonas, or any islander to uncover the plot. "You are to be careful with them - use your imagination, Flach." James, though horrified by Eugene's fate, "to be shot as a spy", will not give in to the Baron's demand that islanders work to extend the runway at the German airbase.

Back at Parliament, Angelique Mahy, who works as the Senator's aide, hints at her knowledge of Phillip's complicity. James' perfunctory denial is interrupted by Flach who needs the Senator's signature on work passes for newly-arrived French prostitutes waiting on the docks. Looking pointedly at Angelique, he implies he is doing the local women a favour by relieving them of the job. When Angelique brings their papers to the dock the guards mistake her for one and Bernhardt, coincidentally on scene, surreptitiously bribes the sergeant to release her.

Felicity engineers a moment alone with the Baron by puncturing her bicycle tyre, and attempts to use his attraction to her as leverage to dissuade him from "murdering" Eugene La Salle. The "death is needed", counters the Baron, to dispel the "cosiness" of the occupation and remind the populace "who has the power and that landsers matter".

His usual methods prohibited by the Baron, and threats having proved ineffective, Flach tries to break Kathleen Jonas' spirit by quarantining her in hospital, under the pretext of transmitting syphilis to German soldiers. Meanwhile, Senator Dorr pleads with Rheingarten, confessing to masterminding the ruse of Eugene's "surrender" and offering his own life in exchange for La Salle's. The Baron refuses and warns him "Don't ever tell Flach what you have just told me".

Over tea Bernhardt opens up to Angelique and makes the argument, both on his own behalf as her suitor, and for millions of young Germans, and English alike:
"We have no choice [in the war], either of us, any of us." (cf "superior orders") "There shouldn't be a war... Hitler has been the worst possible thing for our country". Yet "I [must fight] until it is my turn to die".
She is visibly moved and allows his accidental touch to linger on her hand. By contrast Captain Muller takes a "strictly business" approach to obtaining the companionship of June Mahy: "I pay for my laundry, car repairs, haircuts etc. - I would merely like to pay you for singing at my party"

At La Salle's execution by firing squad, Constable Jonas witnesses Lieutnant Walker administer the coup de grâce and Mr. Brotherson/Phillip, on the grounds to work, hears and is sickened by the shots. The Baron offers his regrets to Felicity, and almost fatherly words of advice to Phillip.

Back at the Mahy shop, war profiteering is in full swing with Cassie, now not above price gouging, is officially the retail side of the operation while Oberwachtmeister Wimmel and Sheldon Leveque handle the supply and distribution. Meanwhile Lieutnant Walker continues to force himself on Zelda, "ordering" her to accompany him to the officers' party at 'Sous la Chenes', (the Dorrs' ancestral home, also doubling as the Baron's HQ) that evening.

That evening at the officers' party, next door to the Dorrs, Von Rheingarten ignores the provocative glances from a young woman and orders Lieutnant Walker not to let any of "that sort go upstairs and mix with the officers". Undeterred, Walker drags a girl into the Dorrs' garden shed and is assaulting her when Felicity makes her presence known, thwarting the rape. Drunk and frustrated he goes to Zelda's flat and sings outside the door until she lets him in. He blames his misbehaviour at the party on her refusal to accompany him, "I am so bloody lonely - I just want a girl that I can respect". She most emphatically tells him that "she is not *that sort* of girl, and if you respect me you'll leave now". After kissing her hand, "I am so glad we are going to get to each other better", he does leave.

Wilf, tasked to drive June home from the party, is sarcastic to the point of cruelty, calling her a trollop, "Party, drinks, singing, dance the night away and paid into the bargain". Inside the house Zelda, is hiding from Walker and June tells them both she doesn't care anymore if anyone, including their mother, thinks she is fraternizing with the enemy. "Say [to her] I spent the evening with a bunch of murderers who just come from shooting Eugene. And tell her how much I enjoyed it."

When the Baron attempts to be cordial towards Mrs. Dorr, and she responds with indignation at his shooting Eugene, he explicitly states another of the series' themes: "That weight of righteousness is very heavy, Mrs. Dorr. Keep up this moral indignation, and come the war's end you'll have drowned in it." The argument escalates and the Baron raises his voice, bringing the Senator who, this time, is ready to fight for his wife.

Wilf, wracked with guilt at being helpless to save, or even comfort Eugene in his last moments of life, is consoled by Kathleen. The next morning Angelique meets Bernhardt at the beach. Resigned to continuing the argument he protests, "I'm not your enemy". This time she takes his hand, "Of course you are, Bernhardt, of course you are". The pair share a kiss.

Episode Five: Unexpected Revelations
In a break from the more comfortable drama of the first four episodes, Director Peter Lydon and writer Stephen Mallatratt show us glimpses of war's extremes: Germany's darkest years, and "Britain's finest hour". Juxtaposing acts of personal heroism and self-sacrifice with despicable institutional cowardice, characters jettison firmly-held principles in the face of economic necessity, and draw upon unimaginable strength to endure the unendurable.

Quick scenes advance the plot lines: Lieutenant Walker, obsessed with Zelda, corners her on the beach and continues to interpret her blunt, even insulting, refusals to see him as playing hard to get. Angelique is unable to face her mother, Cassie, and confess her love for Bernhardt. Senator Dorr must face the grieving parents of Eugene La Salle, but is wracked with guilt and cannot disclose his full role in their son's death. Yet he risks open confrontation with the Baron, who would order the La Salles arrested just for visiting the execution site in the Dorr garden. Mrs. Dorr pleads on the La Salles' behalf. When the Baron's response, "There is no compassion [in war]" visibly, and deeply, hurts her, he offers to "record in which place of unmarked wasteland he's being buried and let [the La Salles] know after the war". Phillip Dorr now feels compelled to complete his mission so that Eugene would not have "died in vain". Angelique receives a note from Bernhardt who, about to go on a raid, promises to drop his bombs "into the sea or on fields".

The tolling of the church bell sets up the reference to Sergei Eisenstein's 1925 masterpiece, The Battleship Potemkin and it's Odessa Steps sequence: the islanders mount an act of nonviolent resistance and convene at the square in front of the German HQ to keep silent vigil and mourn La Salle. It is the second (of three) *moments of decision* for the Baron, who must look down from the balcony into the eyes of those he is about to have shot: Wilf, Felicity and Mr. Brotherson/Phillip. In a brilliant double entendre the vicar, played by Malatratt himself, and James Dorr, simultaneously admire the Baron's "handling of the situation", and step through the "fourth wall" to praise the homage to great Russian director by David Higgs, cinematographer, and Peter Lydon, director.

Sheldon Leveque agrees to help Phillip spy. Cassie has misgivings about taking Oberwachtmeister Wimmel (who doesn't know "whether he is married or not") as her business partner. Constable Jonas turns a blind eye to Kathleen and Sheldon's circumventing German meat-rationing regulations, and states "There's no law anymore - there's just their rules, and that's no law".

Lieutenant Walker forces Zelda to come the cinema with him and watch the infamous Nazi anti-semitic propaganda film, Jud Süß. On screen we see the rape of a Christian woman by the Jew, "Seuss", and his ceremonious lynching. Ironically the "fate-knocking-at-the-door" opening motif of Beethoven's Fifth Symphony has come to represent the European resistance movement, and the islanders voice their disapproval by tapping this rhythm. Walker threatens to have the cinema closed and a last "tap, tap, tap, tap," amuses the film-goers, in stark contrast to the horrors on-screen.

More quick scenes: The Baron plays at being Phillip's father, proudly commenting to Felicity about "Mr. Brotherson's" improvement in wall-building under his tutelage. He admonishes both against further participation in acts of (even) passive resistance. Angelique is distressed by a radio broadcast announcing the RAF's routing of a flight of Heinkels crossing, approaching the coast and shooting down thirty of them over the Channel. June is conflicted: "150 fewer Germans in the islands" yet they're "people too ... young men ... who are not just numbers once you've met them", which, ironically, she urges her sister to do. Over dinner the Jonas' extended family receive word from their daughter, Mary, that she is safe in England, and Wilf and comes to blows with his father-in-law Harry for implying he is "collaborating with the enemy".

Mallatratt re-characterizes Bailiff Francis La Palotte, heretofore portrayed as a well-meaning old man poised to enter dotage, as the poster boy for European complacency at the beginning of the Holocaust. In meeting of the island senate he urges acquiescence to the "German High Command in Paris" who have ordered registration of all Jews on the island, and confiscation of their property. His placating words deeply offend James Dorr, who alone speaks out against the new rules. Director Lydon drives home the point with intercuts of the "debate" and Lieutenant Walker arresting the few Jews that remain on the island.

The other shoe falls when Lieutenant Walker discovers Zelda Kay's true identity as Hannah Kozminsky. After playing cat and mouse with her, he uses the threat of sending her to die in a labour camp as leverage to force her sexual compliance. Cutting from the grotesques of lust, to the tragedy/glory of star-crossed lovers, Angelique discovers that Bernhardt Telleman has survived the ill-fated mission that claimed the lives of his compatriots.

Meanwhile, Walker is searching for Hannah/Zelda who has gone into hiding above Cassie's grocery store. When he suspects Cassie and June of aiding her disappearance the daughter bluffs convincingly, earning her mother's respect for the first time since the occupation. Felicity pleads with Angelique to stop risking her life, and Phillip's, by assisting his espionage and Angelique seizes the moment to profess her love for Bernhardt.

"To favours returned" toasts Oberwachtmeister Wimmel over wine and truffles, a simultaneously clever and tasteless pun: Cassie trades her sexual favours for the economic benefits her association with the German quartermaster supply sergeant brings.

The episode closes with a reference to Anne Frank as Cassie, bringing food to Hannah/Zelda hiding in a secret room above the shop, interrupts her writing in a journal.

Episode Six: Unusual Successes

June is singing for a mixed crowd at the "50/50 Club" which turns ugly when Captain Muller switches places with her regular piano accompanist. Jerrybag! taunts one, throwing a glass that cuts her cheek. The soldiers drag him into the alley where Lieutenant Walker pistol-whips him unconscious. With blood still on his hands, he sits with June imploring her to disclose Hannah/Zelda's location so he can help her assume a new identity.

Meanwhile, Angelique's feelings

have won over her nervousness about sleeping with the enemy and she and Bernhardt rendezvous in Hanna/Zelda's flat. June finds them together, after she ducks in to avoid the derision of islanders who recognised her in the street. Angelique confesses to her sister, "I'm a Jerrybag".

Sheldon accidentally discovers Hannah/Zelda in Cassie's attic hideaway and offers to smuggle her to England with Phillip. Wilf Jonas, having agreed to assist the plot, must find a way to get his fishing boat out of the harbour "without an escort".

Cassie disabuses Oberwachtmeister Wimmel of any romantic delusions regarding their liaison, "It will always be sex, never love...It's the same with any hunger - one might even eat a rat if one were starved."

Senator Dorr's attitude undergoes a sea-change: he expresses a profound hatred of the Germans to Felicity, goes to the La Salles and admits authorship of the plan that got their son shot as a spy, and gives Phillip intelligence about the strength and composition of German forces on the island and their plans to fortify it. Meanwhile, Colin Jonas and his friend Ronald encounter an officer, who drunk and disillusioned, sells his P08 Parabellum for the £5 note Colin got from his uncle, Sheldon Leveque.

The game is afoot as all principals are converging on Nailing Bay where Wilf and Wimmel, aboard the 'Little Mary' have lain at anchor all afternoon but caught only one garfish between them. Sheldon, en route with Hannah/Zelda in his truck improvises cleverly to pass her through a checkpoint without identification papers. When Felicity discovers that Phillip has in fact left for England she is "far more than upset" at James for keeping her in the dark.

Sheldon drops Hannah/Zelda off with Philip but things go wrong with the carefully orchestrated plan when Colin and Ronald, having hiked overland, arrive at Nailing Bay, and see Wimmel and Jonas, who have given up on fishing and are paddling ashore after the motor fails to start. The boys misinterpret Wimmel's posture and gestures with the rifle as an impending execution and shoot at him from the rocks with the pistol. Wimmel, thinking it was a trap to kill him, makes it to the road and commandeers Sheldon's truck to take Wilf to the barracks prison.

That evening the Baron finds Felicity alone with her thoughts on the porch at 'Sous Les Chenes'. Rheingarten has just learned that his youngest son, 'Manfred' in the Luftwaffe, was shot down over the Channel When Felicity reminds him that of Eugene La Salle, he explains, "One only does what one believes is right. In war one has only the *moment of decision*. If I believed it to be right, then it was right. Whoever shot done my son was right." Their shared grief and mutual sympathies linger, complementing the Baron's literate imagery.

Aboard the 'Little Mary' Phillip and Hannah are trying to start the motor but are intercepted by a German cutter before the ignition catches. Hannah jumps overboard seconds before she can spotted by the searchlights but Phillip is taken with the photographs. The Baron visits him in his cell:
"There was a day, you might remember, at the garden wall, when the Senator's wife and you and I, shared a time together. I had the sense that both she and I thought of you as our son, the son both she and I were missing. Oh, Mr. Brotherson, we have talked a lot, I have genuinely enjoyed your company, we have built walls together ... and now we have to shoot you."
Realising that Felicity Dorr is somehow involved, he visits her to personally deliver the news of 'Mr. Brotherson's' capture. Her reaction gives her away; The Baron realises that Mr Brotherson is, in fact, her son. Felicity sheds the last tattered remnants of her dignity and desperately offers her body to him, anything to spare her son.

Hannah, having survived the plunge into the icy channel waters and swam ashore, goes back into hiding above Cassie Mahy's shop.

The Baron is repelled by Flach's suggestion that they just "shoot [Phillip] and have done with it" and orders him instead sent to France as a prisoner of war. He also orders James and Wilf be sent to prison for 6–9 months for assisting him. On the docks Kathleen Jonas says goodbye to her husband. Senator Dorr realising that the Baron's change of heart is due to his wife's efforts, forgives Felicity for "whatever it took" to spare Phillip's life. When Phillip arrives Felicity can only address him as 'Mr. Brotherson' and the ferry departs for Normandy.

Back at 'Sous Les Chenes' the Baron accepts Felicity's thanks with "I've grown sickened, Mrs. Dorr, by the deaths of young men". Angelique comes to Bernhardt and they watch the sunset together.

Response

Overall, the miniseries earned more favourable reviews in the United States than in the United Kingdom. This is possibly due to the near-saturation of British television and film with World War II dramas, and the continuing popularity of the ITV series *Enemy at the Door* (1978–80), which had a similar plot, and *Foyle's War*.

In the Channel Islands themselves, the series faced widespread criticism in the local press due to inaccuracy, mispronunciation of names (for example, 'Mahy' was pronounced 'Mah-hee' rather than the correct 'Ma'yee') and the fact that the series was filmed not on the islands themselves, but the Isle of Man.

Future?

One complaint shared by critics and viewers alike was the lack of resolution at the end of the final episode. Many of the minor plot arcs (i.e. the relationship between the Baron and Felicity; June's tarnished reputation), and some major ones (Zelda's failed escape; Angelique and Bernhardt), were left with loose ends when the mini-series ended. It was rumoured that another batch of episodes was to be produced, possibly taking place months or even years after the original six, and would provide a true ending to the show. This will most likely never occur, however, largely due to the death of writer Stephen Mallatratt.

DVD

The DVD for this series are available, distributed by Acorn Media UK.

Source http://en.wikipedia.org/wiki/Island_at_War

Occupation of the Channel Islands

Occupation of the Channel Islands
Occupation by Germany 1940-45

As part of the Atlantic Wall, between 1945 the occupying German forces and ganisation Todt constructed fortificatio the coasts of the Channel Islands suc observation tower at Les Landes, Jersey

Flag Symbol

Country Channel Islands
State Bailiwick of Jersey Bailiwick Guernsey
Region Channel Islands

Entrance to the German Underground Hospital in Jersey

The **Channel Islands** were occupied by Nazi Germany for much of World War II, from 30 June 1940 until the liberation on 9 May 1945. The Channel Islands are two British Crown dependencies in the English Channel, near the coast of Normandy. The Channel Islands were the only part of the British Isles to be invaded and occupied by German forces during the war.

Before occupation

Demilitarisation

On 11 June 1940, as part of the war effort in the Battle of France, a long range RAF aerial sortie carried out by Whitley bombers against the Italian cities of Turin and Genoa departed from small airfields in Jersey and Guernsey. On 15 June, after the Allied defeat in France, the British government decided that the Channel Islands were of no strategic importance and would not be defended, but did not give Germany this information. Thus despite the reluctance of Prime Minister Winston Churchill, the British government gave up the oldest possession of the Crown "without firing a single shot". The Channel Islands served no purpose to the Germans other than the propaganda value of having occupied some British territory. The "Channel Islands had been demilitarised and declared...'an open town' ".

Evacuation

The British Government consulted the islands' elected government representatives, in order to formulate a policy regarding evacuation. Opinion was divided and, without a policy being imposed on the islands, chaos ensued and different policies were adopted by the different islands. The British Government concluded their best policy was to make available as many ships as possible so that islanders had the option to leave if they wanted to. The authorities in Alderney recommended that all islanders evacuate, and nearly all did so; the Dame of Sark, Sibyl Mary Hathaway, encouraged everyone to stay. Guernsey evacuated all children of school age, giving the parents the option of keeping their children with them, or evacuating with their school. In Jersey, the majority of islanders chose to stay.

Invasion

German soldiers in Jersey.

Since the Germans did not realise that the islands had been demilitarised, they approached them with some caution. Reconnaissance flights were inconclusive. On 28 June 1940, they sent a squadron of bombers over the islands and bombed the harbours of Guernsey and Jersey. In St Peter Port, the main town of Guernsey, some lorries lined up to load tomatoes for export to England were mistaken by the reconnaissance for troop carriers. Forty-four islanders were killed in the raids.

While the German Army was preparing to land an assault force of two battalions to capture the islands, a reconnaissance pilot landed in Guernsey on 30 June and the island officially surrendered to him. Jersey surrendered on 1 July. Alderney, where only a handful of islanders remained, was occupied on 2 July and a small detachment travelled from Guernsey to Sark, which officially surrendered on 4 July.

Occupation

The German forces quickly consolidated their positions. They brought in infantry, established communications and anti-aircraft defences, established an air service with mainland France and rounded up British servicemen on leave.

Government

In Guernsey, the Bailiff, Sir Victor Carey, and the States of Guernsey handed overall control to the German authorities. Day-to-day running of island affairs became the responsibility of a Controlling Committee, chaired by Ambrose Sherwill. Scrip (occupation money) was issued in Guernsey to keep the economy going. German military forces used their own scrip for payment of goods and services.

The German authorities changed the Channel Island time zone from GMT to CET to bring the islands into line with continental Europe, and the rule of the road was also changed to driving on the right.

Alderney concentration camps

The Germans built four concentration camps in Alderney. The camps were subcamps of the Neuengamme concentration camp outside Hamburg and each was named after one of the Frisian Islands: Lager Norderney located at Saye, Lager Borkum at Platte Saline, Lager Sylt near the old telegraph tower at La Foulère and Lager Helgoland in the north west corner of Alderney. The Nazi Organisation Todt operated each subcamp and used forced labour to build bunkers, gun emplacements, air raid shelters, and concrete fortifications. The camps commenced operation in January 1942 and had a total inmate population of about 6,000.

The *Borkum* and *Helgoland* camps were "volunteer" (Hilfswillige) labour camps and the labourers in those camps were treated harshly but marginally better than the inmates at the *Sylt* and *Norderney* camps. The prisoners in *Lager Sylt* and *Lager Norderney* were slave labourers forced to build the many military fortifications and installations throughout Alderney. *Sylt camp* held Jewish forced labourers. *Norderney camp* housed European (mainly Eastern Europeans but including Spaniards) and Soviet forced labourers. *Lager Borkum* was used for German technicians and "volunteers" from different countries of Europe. *Lager Helgoland* was filled with Soviet Organisation Todt workers.

In 1942, *Lager Norderney*, containing Soviet and Polish POWs, and *Lager Sylt*, holding Jews, were placed under the control of the SS Hauptsturmführer Max List. Over 700 of the inmates lost their lives before the camps were closed and the remaining inmates transferred to Germany in 1944.

Resistance and collaboration

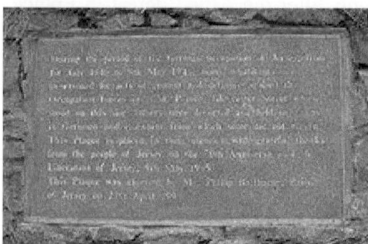

Plaque: *During the period of the German occupation of Jersey, from 1 July 1940 to 9 May 1945, many inhabitants were imprisoned for acts of protest and defiance against the Occupation Forces in H.M. Prison, Gloucester Street which stood on this site. Others were deported and held in camps in Germany and elsewhere from which some did not return.*

There was no resistance movement in the Channel Islands on the scale of that in mainland France. This has been ascribed to a range of factors including the physical separation of the islands, the density of troops (up to one German for every two islanders), the small size of the islands precluding any hiding places for resistance groups and the absence of

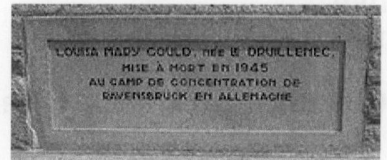

Plaque on war memorial, Saint Ouen, Jersey, to Louisa Mary Gould, victim of Nazi concentration camp Ravensbrück: *Louisa Mary Gould, née Le Druillenec, mise à mort en 1945 au camp de concentration de Ravensbrück en Allemagne.*
Louisa Gould hid a wireless set and sheltered an escaped Soviet prisoner. Betrayed by an informer at the end of 1943, she was arrested and sentenced on 22 June 1944. In August 1944 she was transported to Ravensbrück and murdered in the gas chambers there on 13 February 1945. In 2010 She was posthumously awarded the honour *British Hero of the Holocaust*.

Memorial, St. Helier: *In memoriam: between 1940 and 1945, more than 300 islanders were taken from Jersey to concentration camps and prisons on the continent, for political crimes committed against the German occupying forces.*

the Gestapo from the occupying forces. Moreover, much of the population of military age had already joined the British or French armed forces. Because of the small size of the islands, most resistance involved individuals risking their lives to save someone else.

Resistance involved passive resistance, acts of minor sabotage, sheltering and aiding escaped slave workers (see, for example, *Albert Bedane*) and publishing underground newspapers containing news from BBC Radio. The islanders also joined in Churchill's V sign campaign by daubing the letter 'V' (for Victory) over German signs. A widespread form of passive resistance (albeit taking place in secret within the confines of islanders' homes) was the act of listening to BBC Radio, which was banned in the first few weeks of the occupation and then (surprisingly given the policy elsewhere in Nazi-occupied Europe) tolerated for a period before being once again prohibited. Later the ban became even more draconian, with all radio listening (even to German stations) being banned by the occupiers, a ban backed up by the widespread confiscation of wireless sets. Nevertheless, many islanders successfully hid their radios (or replaced them with homemade crystal sets) and continued listening to the BBC despite the risk of being discovered by the Germans or being informed on by neighbours.

Artists Claude Cahun and Suzanne Malherbe produced anti-German fliers from English-to-German translations of BBC reports, pasted together to create rhythmic poems and harsh criticism. The couple then dressed up and attended many German military events in Jersey, and put the fliers in soldiers' pockets, on their chairs, etc. Some fliers were crumpled up and thrown into cars and windows. In 1944 Cahun and Malherbe were arrested and sentenced to death, but the sentences were never carried out.

A number of islanders, such as Peter Crill, escaped. The number of escapes increased after D-Day, when conditions in the islands worsened as supply routes to the continent were cut off and the desire to join in the liberation of Europe increased.

The policy of the island governments, acting under instructions communicated by the British Government before the occupation, was *passive co-operation*. This has been criticised (see Bunting), particularly with regard to the treatment of Jews. The remaining Jews in the islands, often Church of England members with one or two Jewish grandparents, were subjected to the nine *Orders Pertaining to Measures Against the Jews*, including closing their businesses (or placing them under *Aryan* administration), giving up their wirelesses, and staying indoors for all but one hour per day. These measures were administered by the Bailiff and the Aliens Office.

Some island women fraternised with the occupying forces. This was frowned upon by the majority of islanders, who gave them the derogatory nickname *Jerry-bags*. Records released by the Public Records Office in 1996 suggest that as many as 900 babies of German fathers were born to Jersey women during the occupation.

One side effect of the occupation and local resistance was an increase in the speaking of local languages (Guernésiais in Guernsey and Jèrriais in Jersey). As many of the German soldiers were familiar with both English and French, the indigenous languages enjoyed a brief revival as islanders sought to converse without the Germans understanding.

Stamps designed by Blampied issued in 1943 for use in Jersey during the German Occupation

A shortage of coinage in Jersey (partly caused by occupying troops taking away coins as souvenirs) led to the passing of the *Currency Notes (Jersey) Law* on 29 April 1941. A series of two shilling notes (blue lettering on orange paper) were issued. The law was amended on 29 November 1941 to provide for further issues of notes of various denominations, and a series of banknotes designed by Edmund Blampied was issued by the States of Jersey in denominations of 6 pence (6d), 1, 2 and 10 shillings (10/-) and 1 pound (£1). The 6d note was designed by Blampied in such a way that the word *six* on the reverse incorporated an outsized "X" so that when the note was folded, the result was the resistance symbol "V" for victory. A year later he was asked to design six new postage stamps for the island, in denominations of ½d to 3d. As a sign of resistance, he cleverly incorporated into the design for the 3d stamp the script initials GR (for *Georgius Rex*) on either side of the '3' to display loyalty to King George VI.

British Government reaction

British newspaper dropped on the Islands shortly after the occupation, in September 1940.

The British Government's reaction to the German invasion was muted, with the Ministry of Information issuing a press release shortly after the Germans landed.

On 6 July 1940, 2nd Lieutenant Hubert Nicolle, a Guernseyman serving with the British Army, was dispatched on a fact-finding mission to Guernsey. He was dropped off the south coast of Guernsey by a submarine and rowed ashore in a canoe under cover of night. This was the first of two visits which Nicolle made to the island. Following the second, he missed his rendezvous and was trapped in the island. After a month and a half in hiding, he gave himself up to the German authorities and was sent to a German prisoner-of-war camp.

On the night of 14 July 1940, Operation Ambassador was launched on Guernsey by men drawn from H Troop of No. 3 Commando under John Durnford-Slater and No. 11 Independent Company. The raiders failed to make contact with the German garrison.

In October 1942, there was a British Commando raid on Sark, named Operation Basalt. Four German soldiers were killed and one captured.

In 1943, Vice Admiral Lord Mountbatten proposed a plan to retake the islands named Operation Constellation. The proposed attack was never mounted.

Fortification

Bunker in St Ouen's Bay, Jersey

As part of the Atlantic Wall, between 1940 and 1945 the occupying German forces and the Organisation Todt constructed fortifications, roads and other facilities in the Channel Islands. Much of work was carried out by imported labour, including thousands from the Soviet Union, and under the supervision of the German forces.

The Channel Islands were amongst the most heavily fortified, particularly the island of Alderney which is the closest to France. Hitler had decreed that 10% of the steel and concrete used in the Atlantic Wall go to the Channel Islands. It is often said the Channel Islands were better defended than the Normandy beaches, given the large number of tunnels and bunkers around the Islands. By 1944 in tunneling alone, 244,000 m3 of rock had been extracted collectively from Guernsey, Jersey and Alderney (the majority from Jersey). At the same point in 1944 the entire Atlantic Wall from Norway to the Franco-Spanish border, excluding the Channel Islands, had extracted some 225,000 m3.

Light railways were built in Jersey and Guernsey to supply coastal fortifications. In Jersey, a one-metre gauge line was laid down following the route of the former Jersey Railway from St Helier to La Corbière, with a branch line connecting the stone quarry at Ronez in St John. A 60cm line ran along the west coast, and another was laid out heading east from St Helier to Gorey. The first line was opened in July 1942, the ceremony being disrupted by passively-resisting Jersey spectators. The Alderney Railway was taken over by the Germans who lifted part of the standard gauge line and replaced it with a metre gauge line, worked by two Feldbahn 0-4-0 diesel locomotives. The German railway infrastructure was dismantled after the liberation in 1945.

Many of the bunkers, batteries and tunnels can still be seen today. Some have been restored, such as Battery Lothringen and Ho8, and are open for the general public to visit. After the occupation, the islanders used some of the fortifications for other purposes, but most were stripped out in scrap drives (and by souvenir hunters) and left abandoned. One bunker was transformed into a fish hatchery and a large tunnel complex was made into a mushroom farm.

Deportation

Plaque: *From the rear of this building 1,186 English born residents were deported to Germany in September 1942. In February 1943 a further 89 were deported from another location in St. Helier.*

In 1942, the German authorities announced that all residents of the Channel Islands who were not born in the islands, as well as those men who had served as officers in World War I, were to be deported. The majority of them were transported to the south west of Germany, notably to Ilag V-B at Biberach an der Riss and Ilag VII at Laufen, and Wurzach. This deportation decision came directly from Adolf Hitler, as a reprisal for German civilians in Iran being deported and interned. The ratio was 20 Channel Islanders to be interned for every one German interned. Guernsey nurse Gladys Skillett, who was five months pregnant at the time of her deportation to Biberach, became the first Channel Islander to give birth while in captivity in Germany.

Representation in London

As self-governing Crown Dependencies, the Channel Islands had no elected representatives in the British Parliament. It therefore fell to evacuees and other islanders living in the United Kingdom prior to the occupation to ensure that the islanders were not forgotten. The Jersey Society in London, which had been formed in 1896, provided a focal point for exiled Jerseymen. In 1943, a number of influential Guernseymen living in London formed the Guernsey Society to provide a similar focal point and network for Guernsey exiles. Besides relief work, these groups also undertook studies to plan for economic reconstruction and political reform after the end of the war. The pamphlet *Nos Îles* published in London by a committee of islanders was influential in the 1948 reform of the constitution of the Bailiwick.

Bertram Falle, a Jerseyman, had been elected Member of Parliament (MP) for Portsmouth in 1910. Eight times elected to the House of Commons, in 1934 he was raised to the House of Lords with the title of Lord Portsea. During the occupation he represented the interests of islanders and pressed the British government to relieve their plight, especially after the islands were cut off after D-Day.

Committees of émigré Channel Islanders elsewhere in the British Empire also banded together to provide relief for evacuees. For example, Philippe William Luce (writer and journalist, 1882–1966) founded the Vancouver Channel Islands Society in 1940 to raise money for evacuees.

Under siege

Plaque at Gorey: *Captain Ed Clark, Lieutenant George Haas: On 8 January 1945 these two American officers escaped from their prisoner of war camp in St. Helier. Assisted by local residents and in particular Deputy W.J. Bertram BEM, of East Lynne, Fauvic, they successfully avoided recapture by the German forces. On the night of 19 January 1945 they removed a small boat from this harbour and 15 hours later after an arduous crossing in bad weather, landed near Carteret on the French Cotentin Peninsula. This tablet was unveiled on the 50th anniversary of this event on 20 January 1995 by Sir Peter Crill KBE, Bailiff of Jersey.*

During June 1944, the Allied Forces launched the D-Day landings and the liberation of Normandy. They decided to bypass the Channel Islands due to their heavy fortifications described above. As a result, German supply lines for food and other supplies through France were completely severed. The islanders' food supplies were already dwindling, and this made matters considerably worse - the islanders and German forces alike were on the point of starvation.

Churchill's reaction to the plight of the German garrison was to *"let 'em rot"*, even though this meant that the islanders had to rot with them. It took months of protracted negotiations before the International Red Cross ship SS Vega was permitted to relieve the starving islanders in December 1944, bringing Red Cross food parcels, salt and soap, as well as medical and surgical supplies. The *Vega* made five further trips to the islands before liberation in May 1945.

In 1944, the popular German film actress Lil Dagover arrived to entertain German troops in Jersey and Guernsey with a theatre tour to boost morale.

The Granville Raid occurred on the night of 8-9 March 1945, when a German raiding force from the Channel Islands successfully landed in Allied-occupied France and brought back supplies to their base.

Liberation and legacy

Liberation

Although plans had been drawn up and proposed in 1943 by Vice Admiral Lord Louis Mountbatten for Operation Constellation, a military reconquest of the islands, these plans were never carried out. The Channel Islands were liberated after the German surrender.

Plaque in the Royal Square, St Helier: *On 8 May 1945 from the balcony above Alexander Moncrieff Coutanche, Bailiff of Jersey, announced that the island was to be liberated after five years of German military occupation. On 10 May 1985 Her Royal Highness the Duchess of Kent unveiled this plaque to commemorate the Liberation.*

On 8 May 1945 at 10 am, the islanders were informed by the German authorities that the war was over. Churchill made a radio broadcast at 3pm during which he announced that: *Hostilities will end officially at one minute after midnight to-night, but in the interests of saving lives the "Cease fire" began yesterday to be sounded all along the front, and our dear Channel Islands are also to be freed to-day.*

The following morning, 9 May 1945, HMS *Bulldog* arrived in St Peter Port, Guernsey and the German forces surrendered unconditionally aboard the vessel at dawn. British forces landed in St Peter Port shortly afterwards, greeted by crowds of joyous but malnourished islanders.

HMS *Beagle*, which had set out at the same time from Plymouth, performed a similar role in liberating Jersey. Two naval officers, one of whom was Surgeon Lt Ronald McDonald, were met by the Harbour Master who escorted them to the Harbour Master's Office where they together hoisted the Union Jack, before also raising it on the flagstaff of the Pomme D'Or Hotel. This is re-enacted every year. From 2003 to 2011 Harbour Master and Jerseyman Captain Howard Le Cornu performed this annually. His father John E. Le Cornu and uncle David M. Le Cornu had been in the crowds and had witnessed the occasion on 9 May 1945.

It appears that the first place liberated in Jersey may have been the British General Post Office Jersey repeater station. Mr Warder, a GPO lineman, had been stranded in the island during the occupation. He did not wait for the island to be liberated and went to the repeater station where he informed the German officer in charge that he was taking over the building on behalf of the British Post Office.

Sark was not liberated until 10 May 1945, and the German troops in Alderney did not surrender until 16 May 1945. The German prisoners of war were not removed from Alderney until 20 May 1945, and its population could not start to return until December 1945, after clearing up had been carried out by German troops under British military supervision.

Aftermath

Following the liberation of 1945, allegations of collaboration with the occupying authorities were investigated. By November 1946, the UK Home Secretary was in a position to inform the UK House of Commons that most of the allegations lacked substance and only 12 cases of collaboration were considered for prosecution, but the Director of Public Prosecutions had ruled out prosecutions on insufficient grounds. In particular, it was decided that there were no legal grounds for proceeding against those alleged to have informed to the occupying authorities against their fellow-citizens.

In Jersey and Guernsey, laws were passed to confiscate retrospectively the financial gains made by war profiteers and black marketeers, although these measures also affected those who had made legitimate profits during the years of military occupation.

'Jerry-bags' were women who had fraternized with German soldiers. This had aroused indignation among some citizens. In the hours following the liberation, members of the British liberating forces were obliged to intervene to prevent revenge attacks.

For two years after the liberation, Alderney was operated as a communal farm. Craftsmen were paid by their employers, whilst others were paid by the local government out of the profit from the sales of farm produce. Remaining profits were put aside to repay the British Government for repairing and rebuilding the island. As a result of resentment by the local population about not being allowed to control their own land, the United Kingdom Home Office set up an enquiry that led to the "Government of Alderney Law 1948", which came into force on 1 January 1949. The law provided for an elected States of Alderney, a justice system and, for the first time in Alderney, the imposition of taxes. Due to the small population of Alderney, it was believed that the island could not be self-sufficient in running the airport and the harbour, as well as in providing an acceptable level of services. The taxes were therefore collected into the general Bailiwick of Guernsey revenue funds (at the same rate as Guernsey) and administered by the States of Guernsey. Guernsey became responsible for many governmental functions and services.

Particularly in Guernsey, which evacuated the majority of school-age children ahead of the occupation, the occupation weakened the indigenous culture of the island. Many felt that the children "left as Guerns and returned as English". This was particularly felt in the loss of the local dialect - children who were fluent in Guernesiais when they left, found that after 5 years of non-use they had lost much of the language.

The abandoned German equipment and fortifications posed a serious safety risk and there were many accidents after the occupation resulting in several deaths.

War crime trials

After World War II, a court-martial case was prepared against ex-SS Hauptsturmführer Max List (the former commandant of Lagers Norderney and Sylt), citing atrocities in Alderney. However, he did not stand trial, and is believed to have lived near Hamburg until his death in the 1980s.

Legacy

An inscription, reading "Liberated" in Jèrriais, was installed at La Pièche dé l'Av'nîn in St. Helier to mark the 60th anniversary of the Liberation in 2005

Alderney is still covered in German fortifications built by concentration camp slave labour

Since the end of the occupation, the anniversary of Liberation Day has been celebrated in Jersey and Guernsey on 9 May as a national holiday (see Liberation Day (Jersey)); Sark marks Liberation Day on 10 May. In Alderney there was no official local population to be liberated, so Alderney celebrates "Homecoming Day" on 15 December to commemorate the return of the evacuated population. The first shipload of evacuated citizens from Alderney returned on this day.

Many islanders and evacuees have published their memoirs and diaries of this period.

The Channel Islands Occupation Society was formed in order to study and preserve the history of this period.

The Liberation Jersey International Music Festival was set up in Jersey in 2008 to remember the period of occupation.

A number of documentaries have been made about the Occupation, mixing interviews with participants, both islanders and soldiers, archive footage, photos and manuscripts and modern day filming around the extensive fortifications still in place. These films include: High Tide Productions' *In Toni's Footsteps: The Channel Island Occupation Remembered* - 52min documentary tracing the history of the Occupation following the discovery of a notebook in an attic in Guernsey belonging to a German soldier named Toni Kumpel.

There have also been a number of TV and film dramas set in the occupied islands:

Appointment with Venus, a film set on the fictional island of Armorel (based on the island of Sark).

ITV's *Enemy at the Door*, set in Guernsey and shown between 1978 and 1980

The Eagle Has Landed (1977), directed by John Sturges, had a passage set in Alderney where Radl (Robert Duvall) meets Steiner (Michael Caine).

A&E's *Night of the Fox* (1990), set in Jersey shortly before D-Day in 1944.

ITV's *Island at War* (2004), a drama set in the fictional Channel Island of St Gregory. It was shown by US TV network PBS as part of their *Masterpiece Theatre* series in 2005.

The 2001 film *The Others* starring Nicole Kidman was set in Jersey in 1945 just after the end of the occupation.

A stage play, *Dame of Sark*, by William Douglas-Home, is set in Sark during the German occupation, and is based on the Dame's diaries of this period. It was televised by Anglia Television in 1976, and starred Celia Johnson. It was directed by Alvin Rakoff and adapted for the small screen by David Butler.

The following novels have been set in the German-occupied islands:

Higgins, Jack (1970), *A Game for Heroes*, New York : Berkley, ISBN 0-440-13262-2

Tickell, Jerrard (1976), *Appointment with Venus*, London : Kaye and Ward, ISBN 0-7182-1127-8

Robinson, Derek (1977), *Kramer's War*, London : Hamilton, ISBN 0-241-89578-2

Edwards, G. B. (1981), *The Book of Ebenezer Le Page* (London : Hamish Hamilton, ISBN 0-241-10477-7) includes the Occupation of Guernsey.

Parkin, Lance (1996), *Just War*, New Doctor Who adventures series, Doctor Who Books, ISBN 0-426-20463-8

Binding, Tim (1999), *Island Madness*, London : Picador, ISBN 0-330-35046-3

Link, Charlotte (2000), *Die Rosenzüchterin* [The Rose Breeder], condensed ed., Köln : BMG-Wort, ISBN 3-89830-125-7

Walters, Guy (2005), *The Occupation*, London : Headline, ISBN 0-7553-2066-2

Shaffer, Mary Ann and Barrows, Annie (2008), *The Guernsey Literary and Potato Peel Pie Society*, New York : The Dial Press, ISBN 978-0-385-34099-1

Cone, Libby (2009), *War on the Margins*, London: Duckworth, ISBN 978-0-7156-3876-7

Andrews, Dina (2011), *Tears in the Sand*, Trafford, ISBN 978-1-4269-7006-1

Horlock, Mary (2011), *The Book of Lies*, Cannongate, ISBN 978-1-84767-885-0 - longlisted for the Guardian First Book Award 2011.

The statue in Liberation Square

The Blockhouse, a film starring Peter Sellers and Charles Aznavour, set in occupied France, was filmed in a German bunker in Guernsey in 1973.

A number of German fortifications have been preserved as museums, including the Underground Hospitals built in Jersey (Höhlgangsanlage 8) and Guernsey. Liberation Square in St. Helier, Jersey, is now a focal point of the town, and has a sculpture which celebrates the liberation of the island.

Saint Helier is twinned (since 2002) with Bad Wurzach, where numbers of deported Channel Islanders were interned.

On 9 March 2010 the award of *British Hero of the Holocaust* was made to 25 individuals posthumously, including 4 Jersey people, by the United Kingdom government in recognition of British citizens who assisted in rescuing victims of the Holocaust. The Jersey recipients were Albert Bedane, Louisa Gould, Ivy Forster and Harold Le Druillenec. It was, according to historian Freddie Cohen, the first time that the British Government recognised the heroism of Islanders during the German Occupation.

Source http://en.wikipedia.org/wiki/Occupation_of_the_Channel_Islands

Operation Accumulator

Operation *Accumulator* was an Allied naval operation near the Channel Islands on the night of 12/13 June 1944, in support of Operation *Overlord*, the invasion of France.

As part of Operation *Fortitude*, a series of deception operations had been used to divert attention from the Allied landings by suggesting that a second invasion force was still waiting to land. This caused the defenders to divert their forces from the fighting in Normandy, holding them in reserve for an invasion in the Pas de Calais, to the east.

Some days after the initial landings, it was decided to mount a smaller operation to simulate a follow-up landing force heading for Granville, at the western side of the Cotentin Peninsula. The desired effect would be to force the German command to pull units from the front line and redeploy them to protect the western coast.

The plan was for two Royal Canadian Navy destroyers, *Haida* and *Huron*, to make a series of fake radio transmissions, which would be intercepted. The beginning of the operation went smoothly, with the two ships signalling that the invasion fleet had been delayed by engine problems, and giving a revised plan. However, the radios on the *Haida* broke down, forcing the *Huron* to continue alone; the two ships were also spotted by an Allied reconnaissance plane, which radioed back that it had found "unidentified warships".

The operation was a failure; whilst the signals were made, there was no reaction from the German force. This may have been helped by the Allied air report - a major invasion fleet would have been known to the pilot! - and by a lack of any corroborating evidence; for example, there was no attempt at spoofing radar signals, as had been carried out for the main invasion by Operations *Glimmer* and *Taxable*.

Source http://en.wikipedia.org/wiki/Operation_Accumulator

Operation Ambassador

Operation Ambassador   Part of World War II   **Date**   14–15 July 1940

Operation Ambassador

Location Guernsey
Result British failure
Belligerents
United Kingdom | Germany
Commanders and leaders
Ronnie Tod | Unknown
John Durnford-Slater
Strength
140 | 469
Casualties and losses
1 dead | Unknown
3 captured

Operation Ambassador was an operation carried out by British Commandos on 14–15 July 1940 within the context of the Second World War. It was the second raid by the newly formed British Commandos and was focused upon the German-occupied Channel island of Guernsey.

The raiding party consisted of 40 men from the newly formed No. 3 Commando under the command of Lieutenant Colonel John Durnford-Slater, and 100 men of No.11 Independent Company under Major Ronnie Tod.

Due to a series of mishaps, poor fortune and the haste with which it was planned and implemented, the raid resulted in no immediate military gains for the British, although the experience gained in the mounting and conduct of the operation was to prove invaluable for the success of subsequent Commando operations.

Background

On 30 June 1940 the Germans landed troops on the Channel Islands. Two days later, the British prime minister, Winston Churchill sent a memo to his chief staff officer, General Hastings Ismay, asking him to begin planning an operation for a raid on the islands as soon as possible and stating that he felt that it would be the type of operations that the newly formed Commandos would be suited for. After that, things began moving very quickly. Indeed, the War Office approved the proposal for the raid later that day and shortly after planning began in earnest.

It was decided that a raid by 140 men would land on the island of Guernsey and attack the airfield with the purpose of destroying aircraft and buildings, as well as capturing or killing members of the garrison. The units that were chosen for the raid were 'H' Troop from No. 3 Commando and No. 11 Independent Company. No. 3 Commando, under Lieutenant Colonel John Durnford-Slater, had only just been raised, having completed its recruitment on 5 July, and had not yet begun training, while No. 11 Independent Company under the command of Major Ronnie Tod had been raised earlier in June and had a few weeks earlier undertaken Operation Collar, which had been a hastily organised and largely unsuccessful raid on Boulogne.

During the planning stage, Durnford-Slater went to London where he worked out most of the details with David Niven, who was then serving as a staff officer in the Combined Operations Headquarters.

On the night of 7/8 July a reconnaissance operation was carried out, when Lieutenant Nicolle, an officer in the Hampshire Regiment who was originally from Guernsey, was landed on the island by the submarine HMS H43. Three days later he was picked up and based on the information that he provided it was determined that the garrison on Guernsey consisted of 469 soldiers, concentrated mainly around St. Peter Port and although there were machine gun posts all along the coast, they were sited in a manner that meant that it would take about twenty minutes between an alarm being raised for reinforcements to be dispatched.

Raid

The original plan had been for the raid to be carried out on the night of 12/13 July, however, at the last moment it was put back to 14/15 July. Even then, shortly before embarkation, Durnford-Slater received intelligence that the Germans had reinforced a number of the places where it had been planned to land some of the parties and as such the plan was changed at the last moment. After the details were worked out, final battle preparations were undertaken in the gymnasium at the Royal Naval College, Dartmouth where some of the cadets helped the commandos with loading magazines and helping prepare the Bren guns and Thompson sub-machine guns that had been brought down from London specifically for the operation.

At 17:45 the raiding force embarked upon the two destroyers, *Scimitar* and *Saladin* and accompanied by six Royal Air Force air-sea rescue launches, who would take them from the destroyers to the landing beaches, they set out for the Guernsey.

Under the plan that Durnford-Slater had worked out he had the troops from the independent company attacking the airfield, while the commandos were to create a diversion. To this end, three landing points were selected; however, in the end only the force from No.3 Commando, consisting of only 40 men, was able to land successfully, landing at a beach in Telegraph Bay just west of the Jerbourg Peninsula at 00:50 on 15 July. One party of No.11 were taken to the wrong island (Sark) as a result of a faulty compass, another party crashed into a rock and the other two launches broke down after experiencing a series of technical problems.

Although they managed to get ashore—albeit soaking wet—the party from No. 3 Commando failed to find any of the 469-man German garrison. Despite locating an enemy barracks and a machine gun nest, both had been abandoned by the enemy prior to their arrival. The rendezvous with the destroyers that were picking them up was at 03:00 and if they were late the destroyers were under orders to leave them behind, so the party subsequently returned to the beach, stopping to cut a couple of telegraph lines on the way. Upon arriving at the landing beach, the raiders discovered that they had to extract themselves by swimming some 100 yards (91 m) out to their boats as the tide had risen too high for their motor craft to beach among the rocks.

At this stage it was discovered that three of the men from 'H' Troop, No.

3 Commando could not swim and had to be left on the beach with additional French currency. Although Durnford-Slater requested that a submarine be sent back for these men, the Admiralty decided that it could not take the risk and as a result the men later surrendered. During the extraction, a dinghy was used to ferry weapons to the boats, but on the fifth excursion it was dashed against a rock, possibly drowning one of the three men escorting it.

Aftermath

The raid was ultimately a failure as none of the objectives were achieved by the British. No casualties were inflicted upon the enemy, no prisoners were taken and the only damage inflicted was a cut telephone line. Additionally, the quality of the planning and conduct of the operation has been called into question. Much of the equipment used was either not servicable—faulty compasses, and motor launches that broke down—or inadequate for the job and launches that were unable to come all the way into the beach due to their draught. Also some of the tasks that had been assigned were impractical or had not been rehearsed—the wire intended for use as a road block was too heavy to carry from the beach—and intelligence relating to enemy dispositions upon the island was at best outdated or completely wrong.

Largely this was the result of the haste with which the operation had been conceived and then put together, but it was also indicative of the embryonic status of the raiding and commandos concept.

On the political side, the raid was also a disaster. Churchill was said to have been furious regarding the "comical" way in which the operation was undertaken, and it has been alleged that for some months the whole Commando concept was "in jeopardy", although this did not eventuate. As a concept, the Commandos went on to perform with considerable success later in the war. Indeed, it has been argued, that their future success in operations such as "Overlord" was in part due to the early failures such as "Ambassador" as many lessons were learned as a result of these failures that proved vital in the planning and conduct of future Commando operations.

Nevertheless there were widespread changes. The independent companies were in turn disbanded and their personnel used to raise the first 12 commando units. Much work went into the training and planning side of raiding also, and for the next eight months the commandos did little except train. To this end formalised training schemes and schools were established and Churchill sought to invigorate the concept by replacing General Bourne, who had previously been the Director of Combined Operations with Admiral Sir Roger Keyes.

Source http://en.wikipedia.org/wiki/Operation_Ambassador

Operation Basalt

Operation Basalt
Part of World War II

Ruin of concrete fortification at Saint Ouen, Jersey, dating from German Occupation 1940–45. Sark can be seen on the horizon

Date	October 3 – October 4, 1942
Location	Sark
Result	British victory

Belligerents

 United Kingdom   Germany

Strength

10   20

Casualties and losses

None   four killed, one captured

Operation Basalt was a small British raid conducted during World War II on the German occupied British Channel Island of Sark.

On the night of 3–4 October 1942 ten men of the Special Operations Executive's Small Scale Raiding Force, and No. 12 Commando, landed on Sark with the object of offensive reconnaissance and capturing prisoners.

Nine of the raiders broke into the house of a local while the tenth went to a covert rendezvous with an SOE agent. The occupant of the house, Frances Pittard, proved very informative and advised there were about 20 Germans in the nearby Dixcart Hotel. She also declined an offer to take her back to England.

In front of the hotel was a long hut-type building, apparently unguarded. This annexe comprised a corridor and five rooms wherein were five sleeping Germans, none found to be officers. The men were roused and taken outside whereafter the Commandos decided to go on to the hotel and capture more of the enemy. To minimise the guard left with the captives, the Commandos tied the prisoners' hands with the six-foot toggle ropes each carried, and required them to hold up their trousers. The practice of removing belts and/or braces and tearing open the fly was quite a common technique the Commandos used to make it as difficult as possible for captives to run away.

While this was being undertaken, one prisoner started shouting to alert those in the hotel and was instantly shot dead with a .38 revolver. The enemy now alerted, incoming fire from the hotel became considerable and the raiders elected to return to the beach with the remaining four prisoners. En route, three prisoners made a break. Whether or not some had freed their hands during the firefight is not established nor if all three broke at the same time. Two were believed shot and one stabbed. The fourth was conveyed safely back to England and provided information. The raiders also took with them an SOE agent who had been posing as a Polish worker doing forced labour on the island.

A few days later, the Germans issued a communiqué implying at least one prisoner had escaped and two were shot while resisting having their hands tied. It is believed that this contributed to Hitler's decision to issue his Commando Order instructing all captured Commandos or Commando-type personnel be executed as a matter of procedure.

Names of some of the soldiers on the raid:
Major Geoffrey Appleyard
Captain Philip Pinkney
Lieut. Anders Lassen (later major, VC, MC — see also Operation Roast)
Corporal Flint
Private Redborn
Sargeant Horace 'Brummie' Stokes (later of 2nd SAS - see also Operation Speedwell)

David Niven, who participated in Channel raids, states in his autobiography *The Moon's a Balloon* that the commandos who landed on Sark were taken to the local pub by the locals for a drink. However, Niven also erroneously stated that there were no German troops on Sark at the time.

Source http://en.wikipedia.org/wiki/Operation_Basalt